131
Necessary Conversations
Before Marriage

D0113600

Insightful, highly-caffeinated,
Christ-honoring conversation starters
for dating and engaged couples!

Jed Jurchenko

www.CoffeeShopConversations.com

© 2016 by Jed Jurchenko.

Available from Amazon.com

Insightful, Christ-honoring conversations that every couple should—and must—have before declaring "I do."

Also by Jed

131 Creative Conversations for Couples

131 Engaging Conversations for Couples

131 Conversations That Engage Kids

131 Boredom Busters and Creativity Builders

131 Creative Conversations for Families

131 Stress Busters and Mood Boosters for Kids

131 Conversations for Stepfamily Success

131 Holiday Conversations

131 Conversations for Parents and Teens

Coffee Shop Conversations:
Psychology and the Bible

Coffee Shop Inspirations:
Simple Strategies for Building
Dynamic Leadership and Relationships

Get Free Books

Thank you for purchasing this book! I would love to send you a free bonus gift.

Transform from discouraged and burned out to an enthusiastic agent of joy who leads at a higher, happier level! *Be Happier Now* is easy to apply and is perfect for parents, stepparents, mentors, pastors, coaches, and friends.

Discover practical strategies for staying energized so you can encourage and refresh others. This easy-to-read book will guide you each step of the way!

www.CoffeeShopConverstions.com/happiness

Dedication

To my wife, Jenny:

I cherish the multitude of insightful, fun, and funny date night conversations we had before our marriage.

I treasure the scores of amazing conversations that have taken place since the two of us walked down the aisle.

Thank you for being such a wonderful wife and friend!

Contents

♥ ♥ ♥

♥ ♥ ♥

Introduction

"Some couples put more effort into researching their next vehicle purchase than in getting to know their future spouse."[1] A favorite psychology professor repeated this statement throughout my stint in graduate school. The rest of the class and I would chuckle. The quote has a sarcastic, pessimistic, and outright comical ring to it. *This is just too absurd to be true,* I thought to myself.

Fast-forward ten years. I am a licensed marriage and family therapist and regularly rub shoulders with other professionals in my field. In addition to guiding my clients, I also glean from their stories while continuing to amass valuable life experiences of my own. It is astounding how much personal growth a decade brings! As a result of these experiences, I have concluded that—despite its humorous undertones—my professor's declaration is no joke.

Several key events contributed to this shift in view. First, there are the horror stories recounted by fellow therapists. One colleague described how a couple entered premarital counseling only to discover that while she fervently desires children, he has no interest whatsoever. Even after years of dating and their engagement, this couple had never broached this necessary subject!

Then there is a story from my time serving as a children's pastor. The engaged couple were longtime church members who were well-liked by the pastoral staff. Shortly after the wedding, the husband returned from work to find his bride passed out, drunk. He was utterly shocked. Yet, further conversations with her side of the family revealed that this was a typical pattern of behavior. This new husband had no idea that she was a functional alcoholic until after they walked down the aisle! As you have probably guessed, my friend's marriage did not last. Equally as distressing is the fact that this man's account is not an anomaly. Love stories that spiral into disaster are the reason the phrase "Love is blind" is so common.

Finally, there is the story of my own failed marriage. I hesitate to include this example because I wish it were not the case. I would like to tell you that my story is smooth and clean, but that would be dishonest. During my first engagement, I was naive. I enthusiastically listened with my ears as all the right answers were uttered. Regrettably, I failed to watch with my eyes and to pay attention to that gut feeling that warns when danger is on the horizon. Had I listened at this intense level, I would have understood that the words spoken were not in alignment with my future bride's actions. Sadly, I too became a casualty of blind love.

The Happy Marriage Myth

The idea that true love is the only necessary ingredient for a life of "happily ever after" is a well-rehearsed marriage myth. Walking down the aisle and then driving off to a life of endless bliss only happens in fairytales. The truth is, a happy union requires ongoing, intentional investments and lots of hard work. Love alone—even powerful love—is not a permanent glue that holds a couple together.

In fact, after a couple ties the knot is when the real undertakings begin. Matrimony may be the grandest personal development course that life has to offer. The good news is that although an excellent marriage requires continual effort, it can also be incredibly fun! I can attest to this because I have grown from my past mistakes.

New Beginnings

I knew there was something incredible about Jenny from our very first date. Her gentle smile, compassionate spirit, and the way she insisted that we continue our bayside stroll even after the frigid night air rolled in, instantly won me over. It took me weeks to muster up the courage to ask Jenny for a second date—I was that nervous! My mind whirled a mile a minute as I realized how easy it would be to fall in love with this remarkable woman, and I was not sure that I was ready.

Fortunately, Jenny is patient and was not disheartened by my slow pace. She and I dated for six months before I introduced her to my parents and two daughters. After this, Jenny, the girls, and I began attending church together every Sunday. We spent plenty of time together during the rest of the week too. Then, following a year and a half of dating—going through question books like this one, listening to Jenny's words and observing her actions, an abundance of laughter, countless date-night adventures, and concluding that Jenny was the person I longed to do life with—I popped the question.

Jenny replied with a resounding, "yes," and I was ecstatic! Despite being convinced the two of us were meant to be, Jenny and I spent another thirteen months planning, preparing, and continuing to get to know one another before sealing the deal with the words, "I do."

Four years have passed since that glorious day. Marriage is not always easy, but it is extraordinarily good. While our blended family does not have a fairytale ending — or if such an ending exists, we have yet to find it — there is a deep-rooted contentment that persists through every storm that life sends our way. This joy comes from knowing that Jenny and I are on one another's side and that each of us has the other's best interest at heart. The two of us readily agree that the scores of challenges we have faced have ultimately served to draw us closer. Most importantly, Jenny and I are best friends who truly enjoy being in each other's presence.

Marital Crash Test Dummies

A few years ago, I accompanied a group of teens to a maximum-security prison. After undergoing a thorough search, we were ushered into a cramped conference room. A guard firmly stationed himself in front of the exit. Then a line of lifers—convicts with a life sentence, who demonstrated exceptional behavior and a desire to reach out to troubled teens—filled into the room. One by one, each man took his turn at the microphone and shared the story of his dubious past.

The presentation was as professional as any I have seen. These men commanded respect, connected with their audience, and an intense stillness washed over the room. The session concluded with one inmate pleading with the youth, "Let us be the crash-test dummies. You are here because you are going down the same destructive path we did, but trust me; you do not want to end up like us. Learn from our errors, and do not make the same mistakes."

I want to make a similar plea to you. Let other couples be the marital crash-test dummies. Learn from the many miserable marriages and incredible unions that have come before yours. As you work through the 131 conversations in this book, listen to your partner with your ears, eyes, gut, and heart. Give one hundred times more attention to knowing your spouse than you would give to purchasing your next vehicle. Choose wisely. Then enjoy every moment of your incredible journey together!

Choosing Well

An occupational hazard of being a therapist is hearing many stories of positive and negative therapeutic experiences. Nearly everyone has an impassioned story to tell. One couple recounted how, during premarital sessions, the therapist stated he would try to break up their engagement. The reasoning behind this approach was the idea that if the relationship could withstand the premarital sessions, then it could survive anything. Rest assured, I do not prescribe to this goofy logic.

The aim of this book is neither to encourage nor to discourage your marriage. Instead, my goal is to facilitate insightful and necessary conversations that will allow you to make an informed decision. There are a number of reasons for this. The first is to encourage you and your partner to invest in meaningful conversations that you might not have thought of on your own.

The second goal of this book is to give you permission to ask. You will not find R-rated questions in this book nor inquiries written to embarrass anyone. I hope that these conversation starters make asking the difficult questions — the ones that need to be raised before the wedding — easier. This is a vital step in assuring that the two of you do not become another casualty of blind love.

While dating, Jenny and I worked through a number of conversation books similar to this one. The two of us took turns asking questions in coffee shops, during walks on the beach, and at picnics in the park. Not only did we get to know each other exceedingly well, but it also created an abundance of happy memories that we cherish to this day. This is my final reason for writing this book. My hope is that these conversations generate a multitude of joyful memories in the days ahead.

Trusting the Process

"Trust the process" is another favorite axiom of my graduate school professor and a concluding piece of wisdom in this introduction. As you work through these 131 conversations, commit to slowing down and trusting the process. Do this by creating follow-up questions of your own, answering your partner authentically, and enjoying every moment to the fullest! Allowing these conversations to be a process is what leads to relationship intimacy.

I define intimacy as "into-me-see." It is the ability to know another person while simultaneously being known. Intimacy involves a mutual sharing of inner worlds, including hopes, hurts, dreams, and nightmares. This process of mutual sharing binds hearts together.

Jenny and I know each other better than anyone else does, and we love each other as is—shining successes, dismal failures, and all. My prayer is that this book aids you on your journey toward this deep-rooted, relational joy. So grab a cup of coffee, tea, or other favorite beverage and dive in!

Sincerely,

COFFEE SHOP CONVERSATIONS

Seven Habits of
Miserable Couples

Learn to recognize these miserable habits.
Then, avoid them as you would a rabid dog.

Neither happy relationships nor miserable marriages happen by accident. Both are the result of habits. Happy couples consistently engage in the types of actions that happy couples take. If you and your spouse behave in the ways that happy couples do, soon the feelings will follow. The key to becoming—and staying—a happy couple is to develop healthy, happy habits.

Of course, the opposite is equally as true. Miserable couples behave in the ways that miserable couples do. In other words, misery in marriage also has a predictable and well-worn path. It really is that simple!

This chapter outlines seven deadly relationship habits. As you read this list, take mental notes of any destructive habits infesting your relationship. Then, team up with your partner to exterminate them. One of the easiest ways to accomplish this is to replace the harmful practice with a positive one — such as a habit in the next chapter, which hones in on the seven habits of happy couples. The routines you and your partner practice daily will make or break your marriage.

The Seven Habits of Miserable Couples

1. Miserable couples criticize often.

Criticism is an attack on the other person's character. Instead of saying, "You made a mistake," criticism says, "You are the mistake!" According to relationship expert John Gottman, criticism is a marriage killer. In fact, criticism is so deadly, he refers to it as one of "The Four Horsemen of the Apocalypse."[2] While marital disagreements are a normal part of relationships, attacking your spouse's character is poison.

2. Miserable couples point in blame.

Blaming says, "You caused the problem, and you need to fix it." Because blaming demands the other person take full responsibility for the issue at hand, it obliterates opportunities for collaboration and teamwork. According to Scripture, marriage joins two people together as one. Blaming is deadly because it is a direct attack on marital oneness, and this does neither spouse any good.

3. Miserable couples complain.

Complaining is deadly because it magnifies the problem. In fact, the more a couple complains, the bigger the problem appears. There is a big difference between venting and brainstorming solutions in a reasonable manner. The first adds to problems, while the second seeks to resolve them. Complaining is deadly because it does not seek resolution.

Studies — such as the Bobo Doll experiment — reveal that venting is highly contagious.[3] In this experiment, children observed adults hit and toss around a blow-up BoBo doll through a small window. Next, the child entered the room. The child would naturally reenact the observed behaviors with no prompting required. Parental modeling is powerful! Children soak up negative interactions like a dry sponge and then repeat these patterns in their own relationships.

4. Miserable couples nag.

Nagging is a leaky faucet. Proverbs 27:16 says, "A continual dripping on a rainy day and a contentious wife are alike." There is no doubt in my mind that the same is true for a contentious husband. Do not allow your relationship to die the death of a thousand icy drips. Tighten the faucet of your lips by turning off nagging in your home.

5. Miserable couples make threats.

Threats are especially problematic because they create a catch-22 situation. If the threatened spouse concedes by changing, that spouse is sure to face similar threats in the future — likely the next time the couple reaches an impasse. If the spouse holds firm in the face of peril and the threat is acted upon, additional negativity enters into the relationship. Nothing good ever comes from threats.

6. Miserable couples punish.

Couples who punish build their relationship on fear. Before punishing, ask yourself, "Why would I want to hurt the person I love?" Obviously, there is no good reason to do this. Ultimately, punishments hurt the relationship.

7. Miserable couples bribe to control.

Although bribes are more appealing than threats and punishments, they are one more form of coercion. Bribing is another attempt to get one's spouse to do something that he or she is opposed to doing.

Perhaps you noticed a common theme in these seven habits. Miserable couples seek to control, manipulate, and change their partner. As you work through this book, if there are things about your partner that you cannot accept, make a firm commitment to work through these issues before your wedding day.

Change is tricky, and most couples argue about the same problems throughout their marriage. In my opinion, it is best to either accept your spouse as is or break up before the marriage, than to argue for the remainder of your days on earth.

Happy Couples vs. Miserable Couples

Happy couples team-up. They work together to find win-win solutions. In a happy relationship, partners change out of love for each other. However, compliance is not demanded.

On the other hand, miserable couples put forth great efforts to force change. There is little patience for individual differences. The renowned psychologist William Glasser called these attempts to control our loved ones, external control psychology. Each of the seven habits of miserable couples is an external control psychology tactic.

Scripture opposes eternal control psychology in marriage. One example is found in Philippians 2:4, which states, "Let each of you look not only to his own interests, but also to the interests of others." Miserable couples can move toward a more joyful relationship by putting this Scripture into action.

Now that you know the seven habits of miserable couples, avoid them with gusto. The bottom line is that miserable couples follow a well-trodden path of miserable behaviors. In contrast, happy couples conduct themselves in an equally predictable pattern of happiness. In the next chapter, you will learn seven habits of happy couples. Then, act the way that happy couples do!

Warm-up Conversations

Have you and your partner ever fallen into one of the miserable couples' traps? If so, which ones?

Next time you and your partner begin acting in ways that miserable couples do, what will each of you do differently?

When your spouse catches you engaging in one of these miserable patterns of behavior, how would you like him or her to bring it to your attention?

Seven Habits of Happy Couples

*Essential happy habits to keep
your spouse's love bank full!*

It was a lazy Saturday afternoon. I was in my mid-twenties and lived in a one-bedroom condominium that I had recently purchased. I don't remember why I was rummaging through the junk drawer in my kitchen. I may have been cleaning, or I could have been looking for something I had lost. What I do remember is the feeling of horror that washed over me in the moments that followed.

As I fumbled through the drawer, I found two checkbooks from separate banks. *This is odd,* I thought to myself. Upon closer examination, I realized that one checkbook was linked to my current bank, while the second was connected to an account I had closed a few months prior.

The smart decision would have been to immediately dispose of the old checks after closing the account. Regrettably, I had overlooked this step, and I bet you can guess which account I had written checks out of all week. My heart leaped into my throat, and I felt my face flush with a mixture of embarrassment and anxiety as I grasped the magnitude of my blunder.

How could someone responsible enough to buy his own condo make such an egregious error? I silently wondered. This particular bank charged a hefty fee for every overdraft purchase. I had written seven checks from this closed account, and I knew I was in trouble!

Fixing Mistakes

My lazy Saturday afternoon turned into a scramble. I darted to the bank, explained my predicament, and, fortunately, was able to reinstate my old account before too much damage occurred.

To this day, I remember the gut-wrenching terror that swept over me after discovering I had written checks from a closed account. It is an experience I hope to never repeat.

Yet, as bad as having an overdrawn bank account is, overdrawing from our spouse's love bank is far worse. According to *Stepfamily.org*, one out of two marriages ends in divorce, and the average marriage only lasts seven years.[4] Prior to divorce come feelings of emptiness, hurt, anger, and despair. Divorce is rarely a sudden act. More often, it is the final destination of couples who have amassed a gaping love debt.

The Love Bank Secret

Happy couples keep each other's love bank filled to the brim. The secret to accomplishing this does not stem from massive, one-time love-bank deposits. Instead, happy couples make many smaller deposits daily. Exotic vacations and extravagant acts are added bonuses to an already thriving marriage. This chapter outlines seven habits that will assist you in making love deposits daily.

Each habit is founded on solid psychological principles and aligns with a Biblical worldview. I have a friend who likes to say, "God said it first," because the best techniques that psychology offers are usually a rediscovery of Biblical principles that have been ignored. Listed below, are seven love-bank-filling habits of happy couples, along with Scriptures that highlight the importance of each one.

Seven Habits of Happy Couples

1. Happy couples support each other.

Happy couples strive to be one another's biggest fans. Hebrews 10:24 says, "Let us take thought of how to spur one another on to love and good works." While it is possible to overdo appreciation, this rarely happens.

As a marriage and family therapist, I have never seen — nor heard of — a partner complaining, "My spouse appreciates me too much." So, make your praise sincere and voice your appreciation often.

2. Happy couples encourage.

Ephesians 4:29 says, "You must let no unwholesome word come out of your mouth, but only what is beneficial for the building up of the one in need." Our souls thirst for encouragement as a tree longs for water. For a deep-rooted, flourishing marriage, encourage your spouse daily.

3. Happy couples listen wholeheartedly.

Listening is more than parroting back the last words that fell from your spouse's lips. Heartfelt hearing requires engaged effort. Couples who practice this habit put James 1:19 into action. This passage says, "Let every person be quick to listen, slow to speak, slow to anger." God gave us two ears and one mouth for a reason. Striving to listen to our spouse twice as much as we speak is a good place to begin.

4. Happy couples accept each other's flaws and strengths.

When others accept our weaknesses, we are better able to move on. Surprisingly, the act of acceptance—and not blaming and shaming—is precisely what opens the door to dynamic change and growth. Acceptance is a principle modeled by Christ Himself. Romans 5:8 says, "But God demonstrates his own love for us in this: While we were still sinners, Christ died for us." God accepts you as you are, warts and all. Happy couples follow His lead by accepting their spouse where he or she is at and allowing change to occur over time.

5. Happy couples build trust daily.

Proverbs 28:20 says, "A faithful person will have an abundance of blessings." Happy couples fill each other's love banks by being faithful in the little things. It is during the ordinary days of marriage that extraordinary trust is developed. In short, faithfulness builds trust, and trust is the foundation of a happy marriage!

6. Happy couples demonstrate respect.

Ephesians 5:33 proclaims the value of love and respect within marriage and is the foundational Scripture in the book *Love and Respect*[5]. Author Emerson Eggerichs proposes that men thrive in relationships where respect is shown. As someone who has been a part of countless men's groups and a member of the male species myself, I can attest that respect is an especially big deal for guys.

7. Happy couples negotiate differences.

Proverbs 21:9 states, "It is better to live on a corner of the housetop than in a house in company with a quarrelsome wife." I am sure that the same thing is true for a quarrelsome husband.

In college, therapists discuss the pursue-flee dynamic. This harmful pattern occurs when one partner — who longs for the conflict to end — flees, while the other — desperate to find resolution to the conflict — responds in pursuit. Although the motives of each may be pure, the results are never pretty. Instead of getting stuck in this chaotic relationship dynamic, find a way to negotiate differences and move on.

Creating Win-Win Solutions

You have probably noticed that the seven qualities of happy couples are not one-time strategies, but ongoing attitudes. Couples who integrate these habits into their lives are making continual deposits into their spouse's love bank. This is the best way to make sure one's account is never overdrawn.

Warm-up Conversations

Which love-bank-filling habits are you already practicing?

Which happy habits are an area of potential growth for you and your partner?

Which happy habit fills your own love bank the most?

When I feel like my love bank is nearing empty, how would you like me to let you know?

131
Necessary Conversations
Before Marriage

Chains do not hold marriage together.
It is threads, hundreds of tiny threads which sew
people together through the years.

~ Simone Signoret

And the two will become one flesh.
So they are no longer two, but one flesh.

~ Mark 10:8

Conversation #1

Imagine that a well-known Hollywood producer wants to make a movie about your relationship, and you get to choose the actors. Whom would you select to star as you and your partner? Why?

Conversation #2

If you could travel back in time and relive a part of your relationship, what would it be? What things would you do differently, and what would you keep the same?

Conversation #3

If your loved one wanted to surprise you with your favorite meal, what should he or she cook?

Conversation #4

Describe, in detail, your idea of a perfect romantic evening.

Conversation #5

What small gestures of love are the most meaningful to you? Why?

Conversation #6

How do you think married life will differ from your single life?

Conversation #7

When you were growing up, what did arguments look like in your home?

Conversation #8

When it comes to disagreements, what do you plan on doing similarly to your parents, and what will you do differently?

Conversation #9

What are some of your favorite hobbies and free-time activities?

Conversation #10

Which hobbies and activities will you expect your spouse to participate in with you? How does he or she feel about this?

Conversation #11

How do you think your hobbies will change after marriage? In what ways will they stay the same?

Conversation #12

In your opinion, what are three things that make your partner attractive?

Conversation #13

Why do you want to get married, and why do you want to marry your partner?

Conversation #14

Describe a time the two of you navigated a disagreement successfully. What skills did you use that worked well?

Conversation #15

Think back to one of your more challenging conflicts. What made this disagreement so difficult, and is there anything that you wish you had done differently?

Conversation #16

During a presidential election, would you be more likely to vote for a candidate with the greatest political experience or the candidate with the strongest moral values? Why?

Conversation #17

Which political party do you most closely associate with, and why?

Conversation #18

Does it make any difference to you which political party your spouse endorses? Why or why not?

Conversation #19

Do you want to have children? Why or why not?

Conversation #20

If you plan to have children, how many kids would you like to have, and when would you like to have your first child?

Conversation #21

In your opinion, what are the most important values that parents can teach their children?

Conversation #22

What is your favorite holiday, and how do you celebrate it?

Conversation #23

Are there any holidays that you don't celebrate? If so, why not?

Conversation #24

Do you prescribe to a particular faith? If so, on a scale of 1-10, how important is your faith to you? (1 is not very important, and 10 is incredibly important.)

Conversation #25

Does it matter if your partner shares your faith or values? Why or why not?

Conversation #26

Growing up, what faith-based traditions were important in your family? (For example, did you attend church weekly, go through confirmation, get baptized, pray before meals, etc.)

Marriage is an alliance entered into by a man who can't sleep with the window shut, and a woman who can't sleep with the window open.
~ George Bernard Shaw

44

Conversation #27

What role will faith play in your new family? Will this role change after having children?

Conversation #28

What kind of discipline was implemented in your home when you were a child?

Conversation #29

When you have children, what will discipline look like in your new family, and who will be responsible for implementing it?

Conversation #30

Who are some of your closest friends, and why are these friendships important to you?

Conversation #31

How will your relationships with your friends change after you are married?

Conversation #32

Regarding finances, are you a saver or a spender? As a bonus, tell a story that illustrates your saving and spending habits.

Conversation #33

How many credit cards do you have? What is your total credit card debt?

Conversation #34

Growing up, what were your parents' views toward money? Were they more likely to save, spend, plan, etc.?

Conversation #35

How will your new family manage money similarly and differently than your parents did?

Conversation #36

Will the two of you have separate or joint bank accounts? Why?

Conversation #37

What types of purchases will you and your spouse talk about beforehand, and which purchases will you make without prior discussion?

True love stories never have endings.
~ Richard Bach

Conversation #38

Once you are married, where will the two of you live?

Conversation #39

Would you ever consider living in a different state or country? For what reasons would you be willing to move?

Conversation #40

Using as much detail as possible, describe your ideal home. Where is it located? How many rooms are there? What is the yard like, etc.?

Conversation #41

Do you plan to attend college or trade school in the future? If so, how does your partner feel about this?

Conversation #42

Who is the happiest couple that you know? In your opinion, what makes this couple's relationship work so well?

Conversation #43

On a scale of 1-10, with 1 being miserable and 10 being ecstatic, how happy are you at your present job? Why?

Conversation #44

Where do you picture yourself working ten years from now?

Conversation #45

Imagine you peer into a crystal ball and see a glimpse of your family ten years in the future. Describe what you see.

Conversation #46

What do you think are the key ingredients necessary for a lifetime of love?

Conversation #47

Growing up, what household tasks did your dad take responsibility for, and which did your mom do? How well did these family roles work for them?

*God is more interested in your future
and your relationships than you are.*
~ Billy Graham

Conversation #48

Regarding roles and responsibilities at home, what would you do similarly to your family of origin, and what things would you like to do differently?

Conversation #49

Do you believe in traditional or non-traditional gender roles in the home? For example, would you want the husband to work while the wife takes the primary role in raising the children or vice versa?

Conversation #50

Do you consider yourself a morning person or a night person? If you and your spouse differ, how might you navigate this?

Conversation #51

In your opinion, is divorce ever justified? If so, what would be viable reasons for getting a divorce?

Love one another and you will be happy.
It's as simple and as difficult as that.
~ Michael Leunig

Conversation #52

What is a favorite holiday memory that you and your partner have together? What makes this memory so special to you?

Conversation #53

After marriage, how will you divide the holidays between your families? Will you celebrate as a couple, with one or both sets of parents, create a rotating schedule, etc.?

Conversation #54

What is a favorite memory of a family vacation?

Conversation #55

What types of vacations do you hope to take in the future?

Conversation #56

Do you see yourself always working, being a homemaker, or retiring early? How does your partner feel about this?

Conversation #57

Are there any household tasks such as cooking, laundry, paying bills, etc., that you do not do, either because you choose not to do them or because you don't know how to do them?

Conversation #58

Do you like to keep your home organized or are you fine with a creative mess?

Conversation #59

Do you consider yourself an affectionate person? Why or why not?

Conversation #60

They say, "Opposites attract." What are some opposites that you find attractive in your partner?

Conversation #61

What are some differences your partner has that you find annoying? How will the two of you negotiate these differences?

Conversation #62

If there were an unexpected pregnancy, would you or your spouse ever consider an abortion? Why or why not?

Conversation #63

According to statistics, nearly half of first marriages end in divorce. Why do you think this is the case?

Conversation #64

What are some reasons that your marriage will succeed? (You may want to team up and list ten reasons that your marriage will defy the odds.)

Conversation #65

When you and your spouse go through challenging times, to whom will you look for wisdom and support?

Conversation #66

Imagine you are having a horrendous day. How would you like your spouse to comfort and encourage you?

Conversation #67

Once married, will you share email and social media accounts or keep them separate? Why?

Conversation #68

What is one of your favorite nonfiction books, and what was your biggest takeaway?

Conversation #69

What is a favorite fiction book? What was it about the story that caught your interest?

Conversation #70

If your relationship was a book, what section of the bookstore would it be placed in, and why? (For example, drama, comedy, steamy romance, tragedy, etc.)

Conversation #71

What is something that you are doing to grow as a person this year?

For it was not into my ear you whispered,
but into my heart.
~ Judy Garland

Conversation #72

How would you like your partner to support you in your personal growth?

Conversation #73

When you feel stressed out, what helps you to relax?

Conversation #74

Growing up, what were your parents' attitudes toward alcohol? (Were they teetotalers, casual drinkers, alcoholics, in recovery, etc.?)

Conversation #75

What will the attitude toward alcohol be in your new home?

Conversation #76

What is the most alcohol you ever drank in a day? What, if anything, did you learn from the experience?

Conversation #77

What adventures would you like to have with your future spouse?

Conversation #78

On a scale of 1-10, how adventurous are you? A 1 means "Watching *The Discovery Channel* on tv is as adventurous as it gets." 10 means "Skydiving, chocolate-covered bacon, and scuba diving; you name it, and I'll do it!"

Conversation #79

What has been one of your favorite adventures together so far, and what made this time so special?

Conversation #80

Have you ever used drugs (including marijuana or prescription pills), and what is your current attitude toward casual drug use?

Conversation #81

What television series are you currently watching, and what do you like about it?

Conversation #82

When you were a child, what were some of the house rules?

Conversation #83

What is one rule that was helpful, and what is one rule that could have been better?

Conversation #84

What are some house rules you hope to implement in your own home—both immediately and after you have children?

Conversation #85

When you are sick, how would you like your spouse to care for you?

Conversation #86

What has been one of your favorite romantic dates together so far? What made this time so meaningful?

Conversation #87

What are some of the relationship skills you are using to make your friendship work well?

Conversation #88

What are some of the best ways your partner shows you that he or she cares?

Conversation #89

Are there any lingering physical or mental health issues that you have not told your spouse about? If so, what are they?

Conversation #90

Have you ever been arrested? If so, what is the story behind the arrest, and what did you learn from it?

Conversation #91

Growing up, how often did your family attend church services together?

Conversation #92

How often will the two of you attend church once you are married?

Conversation #93

If Jesus were to ask you, "Who do you say that I am?" how would you answer and why?

Conversation #94

On a scale of 1-10, how happy are you with your physical appearance, and why?

Conversation #95

What would you like your new family culture to be like? In what ways will it be similar to your old family culture, and how will it differ?

Conversation #96

Every family has a unique culture in their home. Describe what your family culture was like when you were growing up?

Conversation #97

If you could change one thing about your physical appearance, what would it be and why?

Conversation #98

What is the worst injury you ever had, and how did it happen?

Conversation #99

If you and your spouse were in an especially rough patch in your marriage, would you be willing to attend couple's counseling? Why or why not?

Conversation #100

Will you stay in contact with old girlfriends or boyfriends after marriage? How does your partner feel about this?

Conversation #101

What are a few of life's simple pleasures that bring you joy?

Conversation #102

Growing up, how were problems addressed in your family? Were they ignored, shouted, discussed, etc.?

Conversation #103

What would make it difficult for you to share a current problem with your spouse?

Conversation #104

If your partner sees that you are upset and have shut down, how would you like him or her to draw you out?

Conversation #105

What do you picture your relationship with your new in-laws being like?

Conversation #106

Describe what your ideal wedding day looks like?

Conversation #107

Imagine that you find a magic lamp on your wedding day. The genie inside offers to grant you three wishes for your marriage. Working together, what do you and your spouse wish for?

Conversation #108

If you knew that you were about to be stranded on a deserted island and had the opportunity to take one luxury item with you, what would you bring?

Conversation #109

Would you rather have a large wedding or a small wedding? Why?

Conversation #110

In your opinion, how important is the wedding day to your overall relationship? Does an amazing wedding create a better marriage?

Conversation #111

How important is the wedding day to you personally, and why?

Conversation #112

What spiritual activities will the two of you engage in as a couple?

Conversation #113

Describe a time when God answered your prayer. What did you pray for, and how did God provide?

Conversation #114

When was the last time you prayed, and what did you pray about?

Conversation #115

What are some ways that your partner can pray for you?

Conversation #116

What song best describes your relationship, and why?

Conversation #117

Do you ever lay awake at nite worried? If so, what causes you to stress?

Conversation #118

What character qualities do you find especially attractive in your loved one, and why?

Conversation #119

On a scale of 1-10, how much do you enjoy spending time with your spouse's friends? 10 means, "I love it. They are the best!" A 1 means, "Help! Get me away from these crazy people, please!"

Conversation #120

What is one quote or piece of advice that you try to live by? Why does this statement resonate with you?

Conversation #121

If you could travel back in time and ask one Biblical figure for marriage advice, who would you meet with, and what would you ask?

Conversation #122

If you could travel back in time and ask one historical figure (outside of the Bible) for marriage advice, who would you meet with, and what would you ask?

Conversation #123

What makes you nervous about marriage?

Conversation #124

What gets you excited about being married?

Conversation #125

What was your favorite childhood pet, and what is a favorite pet memory?

Conversation #126

Would you ever want to own a pet or pets? If so, what kind and how many?

Conversation #127

Describe some beloved Christmas traditions. Which customs do you plan to carry over into your new family?

Conversation #128

Describe some of your favorite Thanksgiving traditions. Which ones do you plan to carry over into your new family?

Conversation #129

Do you find it easy or difficult to be thankful? Why do you think this is?

Conversation #130

What is the most insightful thing you learned about your partner while going through the questions in this book?

Conversation #131

Now that you have completed these questions, how will the two of you you continue to foster a spirit of into-me-see?

Seven Habits for After Tying the Knot

Happy habits for a vibrant marriage!

Happy couples keep the loving actions going after they are married. Sometimes, when my younger brother asks me what my plans are for the weekend, I jokingly reply, "I'm going to lay on the couch, watch action movies, and eat junk food all weekend long. I've attracted my wife, so there is no reason to stay in shape or to go out anymore." Before judging me too harshly, rest assured that this is not something I would actually do.

I love spending time with Jenny and our daughters. In fact, it is my absolute favorite thing to do! A day at the beach, walks to the park, and family meals are far more appealing to me than zoning out in front of the television. I am well aware that happily-married couples continue to actively engage in the happy marriage habits they created before the wedding.

Sadly, some couples live out my sarcastic joke. This final chapter is a gentle reminder to keep love going after tying the knot.

Seven Habits for After Tying the Knot

1. Keep putting your best foot forward.

While dating, couples are on their best behavior. They listen attentively, laugh at each other's jokes, and choose to believe the best about each other. Married couples tend to be more honest, raw, and real. While this can be good — because raw emotions and serious conversations add much to the relationship — don't forget to put your best foot forward, too. Marriage is not an excuse for relational laziness. Happy couples put their best foot forward day after day.

2. Catch foxes.

Song of Solomon 2:15 says, "Catch for us the foxes, the little foxes that ruin the vineyards, our vineyards that are in bloom." "Catch the little foxes" is another way of saying, "Get rid of small grudges." Tiny foxes ruin a vineyard, and small bitterness will fester and spoil a marriage. The second happy-marriage habit is to choose to see the best in your spouse by letting the small stuff go!

3. Have fun.

Dating is fun, and marriage needs to be fun, too. Don't stop laughing, joking, and having fun together after the wedding. Marriage does not need to be fun all the time, but it must be fun some of the time. What actions are you taking to keep the joy in your relationship alive?

4. Keep saying, "I love you."

I once heard a story about a wife who asked her husband, "Do you still love me?" The husband replied, "Honey, I told you I loved you on our wedding day, and if anything changes, I will let you know." Do not be this couple!

Proclamations of "I love you" should abound, along with plenty of words of affirmation and caring actions to back them up. While it is true that "love is a verb that must be demonstrated with actions," the vocabulary is still essential. Refine the art of speaking and demonstrating love in your relationship.

5. Fill your spouse's love bank daily.

Imagine a rich uncle offers you a gift of a million dollars today or the gift of a penny a day, doubled every day for the next thirty days. Which would you choose?

If you have heard this before—or if you took the time to do the math—then you know to go for the penny. A penny a day, doubled every day for thirty days, starts small. However, by day thirty, you would receive $5,368,709.10. When you add this to what you collected over the previous twenty-nine days, you have amassed the grand total of $10,737,418.23. The point of the story is that small investments compound over time and produce big results. This is true in finances, and it is true with love. Make small love investments daily and watch your love grow over time.

6. Keep dating.

Dating is more challenging after marriage and even more so after children. However, don't let this stop you. Difficulties only mean that more creativity is required. Set a regular date night, and find a good babysitter. In addition, learn how to engage in date night activities after the kiddos fall asleep—because after kids, sometimes a night on the town takes up too much energy. With creativity and practice, dating can be even more fun after the wedding!

7. Ask good questions.

Happy couples stay curious. Remember, intimacy is into-me-see. You and your spouse are continually changing. There will always be new things to learn about each other, so keep talking and stay curious. May your marriage overflow with happiness and love in the years ahead!

Concluding Conversations

Which of these happy marriage habits are you good at?

Which habits do you need to continue growing in?

Are there any habits you would add to this list?

End Notes

1. Quote credited to Dr. Barry Lord.

2. Gottman, John and Silver, Nan. *The Seven Principles For Making Marriage Work*, Harmony, 2015.

3. Information on this popular experiment is readily available. You can find more on Wikipedia at:
   https://en.wikipedia.org/wiki/Bobo_doll _experiment

4. *Stepfamily Statistics. Retrieved from:* http://www.stepfamily.org/stepfamily-statistics.html

5. Eggerichs, Emerson. *Love and Respect, Thomas Nelson,* 2004.

Thumbs Up
or Thumbs Down

Thank you for purchasing this book!

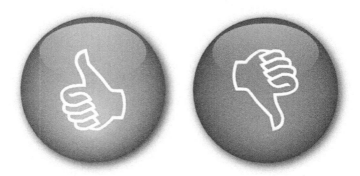

I would love to hear from you! Your feedback not only helps me grow as a writer, but it also helps me to get books into the hands of those who need them most. Online reviews are one of the biggest ways that independent authors — like me — connect with new readers.

If you loved the book, could you please share your experience? Leaving feedback is as easy as answering any of these questions:

- What did you like about the book?
- What is your most important takeaway or insight?
- What have you done different — or what will you do differently — because of what you have read?
- To whom would you recommend this book?

Of course, I'm looking for honest reviews. So, if you have a minute to share your experience, good or bad, I would appreciate it.

I look forward to hearing from you!

Sincerely,

COFFEE SHOP CONVERSATIONS

About the Author

Jed Jurchenko is a husband, father to four girls, a psychology professor, and a therapist. He supports passionate Christ-followers in leading their families, growing their friendships, and maturing their faith so that they can live joy-filled, Christ-honoring lives.

Jed graduated from Southern California Seminary with a Master of Divinity and returned to complete a second master's degree in psychology. In their free time, Jed and Jenny enjoy walking on the beach, reading, and spending time together as a family.

Continue the Conversation

If you enjoyed this book, I would love it if you would leave a review on Amazon. Since I am a new author, your feedback is a huge encouragement and helps books like this one get noticed. It only takes a minute, and every review is greatly appreciated. Oh, and please feel free to stay in touch too!

E-mail: jed@coffeeshopconversations.com

Twitter: @jjurchenko

Facebook: Coffee Shop Conversations

More Creative Conversations

This book and other creative conversation starters are available at www.Amazon.com.

Take your relationship from bland to inspired, passionate, and connected as you grow your insights into your spouse's inner world! Whether you are newly dating or nearing your golden anniversary, these questions are for you! This book will help you share your heart and dive into your partner's inner world.

131 Creative Conversations for Couples

More Creative Conversations

These creative conversation starters will inspire your kids to pause their electronics, grow their social skills, and develop lifelong relationships!

This book is for children and tweens who desire to build face-to-face connections and everyone who wants to help their kids to connect in an increasingly disconnected world. Get your kids talking with this activity book the entire family will enjoy.

131 Conversations That Engage Kids

Made in the USA
Monee, IL
28 March 2022

93688541R00046